Life Stories
Grace Darling

Clare Chandler

Illustrated by Barbara Loftus

WAYLAND

Life Stories

Louis Braille
Christopher Columbus
Grace Darling
Guy Fawkes
Anne Frank
Gandhi
Helen Keller
Martin Luther King
Nelson Mandela
Florence Nightingale
Shakespeare
Mother Teresa

Cover and title page photograph: One of the many portraits of Grace Darling.
Cover illustration: The famous rescue of 1838.

Editor: Polly Goodman
Designer: Joyce Chester

First published in 1995 by
Wayland (Publishers) Ltd
61 Western Road, Hove
East Sussex BN3 1JD, England

British Library Cataloguing in Publication Data
Chandler, Clare
Grace Darling. – (Life Stories)
I. Title II. Loftus, Barbara III. Series
942.07092

ISBN 0 7502 1618 2

Typeset in England by Joyce Chester
Printed and bound in Italy by G. Canale and C.S.p.A., Turin

Contents

Words in **bold** are explained in the glossary on page 30.

A Darling girl

On 24 November 1815 in the village of Bamburgh, a baby girl was born. Her parents, William and Thomasin Darling, already had six children. But they were pleased that their baby was born healthy and beautiful. They called her Grace and added Horsley, her mother's **maiden name**.

▲ This is Bamburgh village and its castle today.

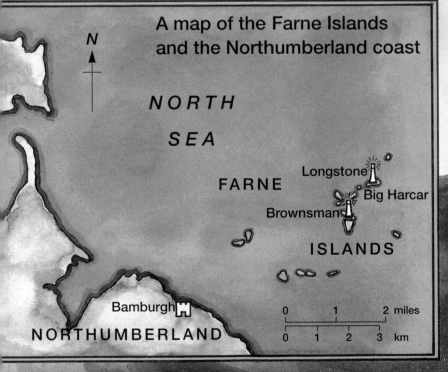

A map of the Farne Islands and the Northumberland coast

N

NORTH

SEA

FARNE

Longstone

Big Harcar

Brownsman

ISLANDS

Bamburgh

NORTHUMBERLAND

0   1   2 miles

0   1   2   3   km

4

The village of Bamburgh is on the east coast of Northumberland. It looks out towards the Farne Islands, a group of craggy rocks. The seas are wild here. So in order to warn ships of the dangers, there was a **lighthouse** on the island of Brownsman.

Grace's father was the lighthouse keeper, the person who made sure the lighthouse lantern was lit and watched out for boats in trouble at sea.

Ships sail past Longstone Lighthouse in the nineteenth century. ▼

5

Growing up on an island

When Grace was three weeks old, she was taken back to the island of Brownsman where her family lived. They lived in a small cottage attached to the lighthouse there. Two years later, Grace's mother had twin boys. Grace lived on Brownsman Island with her parents and eight brothers and sisters for the first ten years of her life.

The Darling family were the only people who lived on the island. Their cottage had no running water or electricity. But it had a pond and a walled garden where they kept chickens and grew their own vegetables and flowers.

Grace loved the sea-birds that she saw around the island. She would watch the puffins, razor-bills and guillemots and she wrote down the birds she saw and how they behaved in a **journal**.

▲ The remains of the cottage and Brownsman lighthouse today.

When Grace was five, she had a pet eider-duck which would follow her everywhere and would feed from her hand.

Life in a lighthouse

Unfortunately, the lighthouse at Brownsman Island was not in a good position for guiding ships past the dangerous rocks. So a new lighthouse was built at Longstone, the furthest island from the mainland. Longstone was a bare rock, many kilometres from the shore, without a blade of grass growing on it. In 1826 the Darling family moved to the new lighthouse.

▲ Longstone Lighthouse on its bleak island.

Grace and her family spent most of their time on the ground floor of the lighthouse. This was a large room, heated by a wood stove, which was their kitchen and dining room as well as their living room. Above that, a **spiral staircase** led to three circular bedrooms, one above the other. Grace's bedroom was on the third floor. At the top was the lighthouse's lantern.

◄ A cross-section of the Longstone Lighthouse. The kitchen is on the ground floor. A spiral staircase leads up to three bedrooms, one above the other.

Mr and Mrs Darling taught their children to read and write. Grace and her sisters also learnt to knit, **spin** and sew. Her father was very strict about his children's education. He thought that reading story books and plays was a waste of time. So they were only allowed to read books about religion, history and geography.

Grace was kept busy all day with her studies, needlework and keeping the house clean and tidy. Sometimes, when her brothers were not there, she would help her father when he went out in the boat. Grace also took her turn at the top of the lighthouse keeping watch, day and night, for ships in trouble at sea.

▲ Grace standing on Longstone Island.

The lookout

From her lookout post at the top of the lighthouse, Grace saw many ships passing by. She loved to watch the great sailing ships on a fine day, with their tall masts and huge white sails. As she grew older, though, she saw a different type of ship. These new boats had short masts and funnels which let out clouds of black smoke. They were **paddle-steamers** and they were run by **steam engines**.

Grace lived at a time when there was a great deal of excitement about steam engines. These new engines

▲ Steam trains like this made travel much quicker and cheaper.

made a great difference to people's lives. While Grace was a girl, the first trains started running and railway tracks were being laid all over Britain. The Darlings saw none of this from their lighthouse, but it was exciting to see the **steamships** going by.

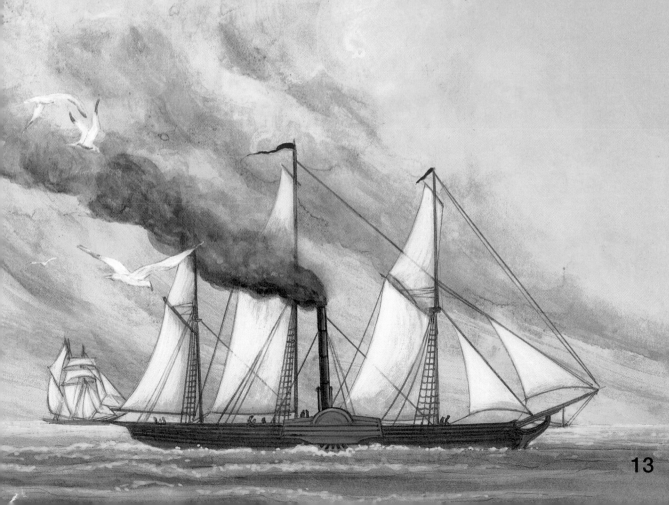

The wreck

On a stormy night in September, 1838, a paddle-steamer called the *Forfarshire* ran into trouble near the Darlings' lighthouse. Its engines stopped working and it was blown on to the Big Harcar rock. Within fifteen minutes the ship had broken in two. The back half was swept away and sank, with over forty-eight people on board.

◄ A painting of the *Forfarshire* as it set off on its last journey. You can see the big wheels, or paddles, at the side which moved it along.

But the front half, which included the front mast, funnel, paddles and engines, was left jammed on the rock. Only twelve people were left on the wreck, including five **crew** members.

As the morning came, a few of the survivors managed to scramble from the wreck on to the rock. There they clung on, desperately hoping someone would see them.

The rescue

The next morning, as soon as it was light enough to see clearly, Grace and her father spotted movements on the Big Harcar rock. Grace was now twenty-two and all her brothers and sisters had left the lighthouse to live on the **mainland**. There was no one to help her father row the boat to rescue the people stranded on the rock. So Grace decided that she would go with him.

▲ The boat which Grace and her father used in the rescue.

Grace and her father each took an oar and rowed out to the Big Harcar, about a kilometre away. The sea was still rough and as they reached the rock the waves rocked the boat from side to side. Mr Darling leapt out of the boat and on to the rock while Grace kept on rowing backwards and forwards nearby, trying to keep the boat from being dashed against the reef.

They found nine survivors on the rock. There were four crew members and five passengers. The only woman, Mrs Dawson, was holding her two small children who had died in her arms. Grace's father helped Mrs Dawson and four of the men into the boat and then rowed back to the lighthouse. There, Grace's mother was waiting for them.

Grace's father and two of the *Forfarshire* crew then went back for the other four men still waiting on the Big Harcar. Meanwhile, Grace and her mother looked after and comforted the injured and shocked survivors. The sea was still very rough. So they all had to stay in the lighthouse for three days until it was calm enough for the little boat to reach the mainland.

Fame and glory

Soon the story of the wreck and the daring rescue was on the front pages of all the newspapers. And Grace Darling became a **heroine**. Everyone wanted to know all about Grace, especially what she looked like. Since there were no televisions or cameras in Britain in those days, lots of artists came to the lighthouse to paint Grace's portrait instead.

▲ A portrait of Grace Darling. At least twelve artists came to the lighthouse to paint her.

For years after the rescue, the lighthouse was busy with visitors who wanted to see the famous Darling father and daughter. Many were surprised when they saw Grace. They had expected her to be very tall and strong. Instead they found a small young woman with a lovely smile.

Grace was sent hundreds of letters and presents as well as money from well-wishers. She was often asked for a lock of her hair for people to remember her by. People presented her with medals for her bravery and even Queen Victoria sent her £50.

However, Grace did not enjoy all this attention. She found that writing thank-you letters and sitting still for portraits left her little time for her usual work.

Boat-loads of visitors arrive at the lighthouse to see Grace. ▼

The Duke

Not far from Bamburgh was Alnwick Castle, home of the Duke of Northumberland. The Duke was president of the Royal Humane Society. This group rewarded people who showed great bravery saving other people's lives.

▲ A photograph of Alnwick Castle today, taken from above.

When he heard the story of the rescue, the Duke awarded a gold medal to both Grace and her father. He invited them to Alnwick Castle to give them their medals. Then he told them that he had decided to become Grace's **guardian**.

Grace had been given about £700 in presents. This was a small fortune in those days, and the Duke said he would look after the money for her.

The Duke kept up his interest in Grace, sending her money when she needed it, and giving her presents for her family at Christmas.

The Duke of Northumberland gives Grace and her father a gold medal for their bravery. ▼

23

A serious illness

In April 1842, only four years after the famous rescue, Grace became ill. She felt weak and feverish and had a cough that would not go away. Eventually, she went to stay with her sister in Bamburgh so that she would be near the family doctor. When Grace did not improve, her sister, Thomasin, gave up her job as a **seamstress** so that she could nurse Grace.

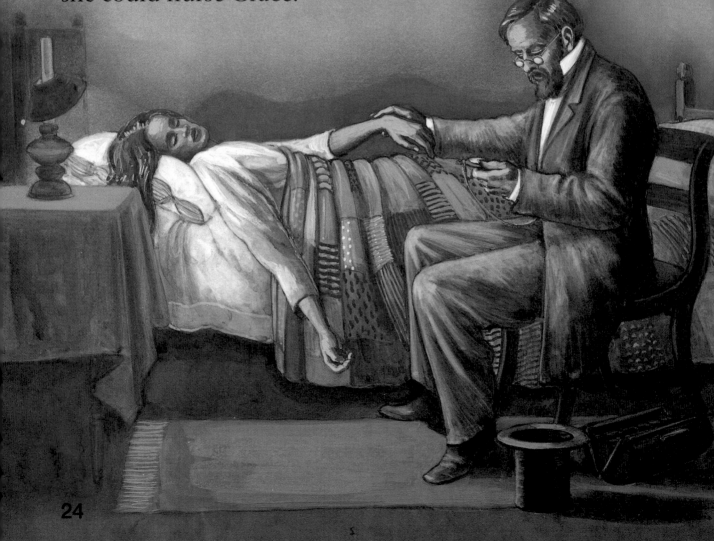

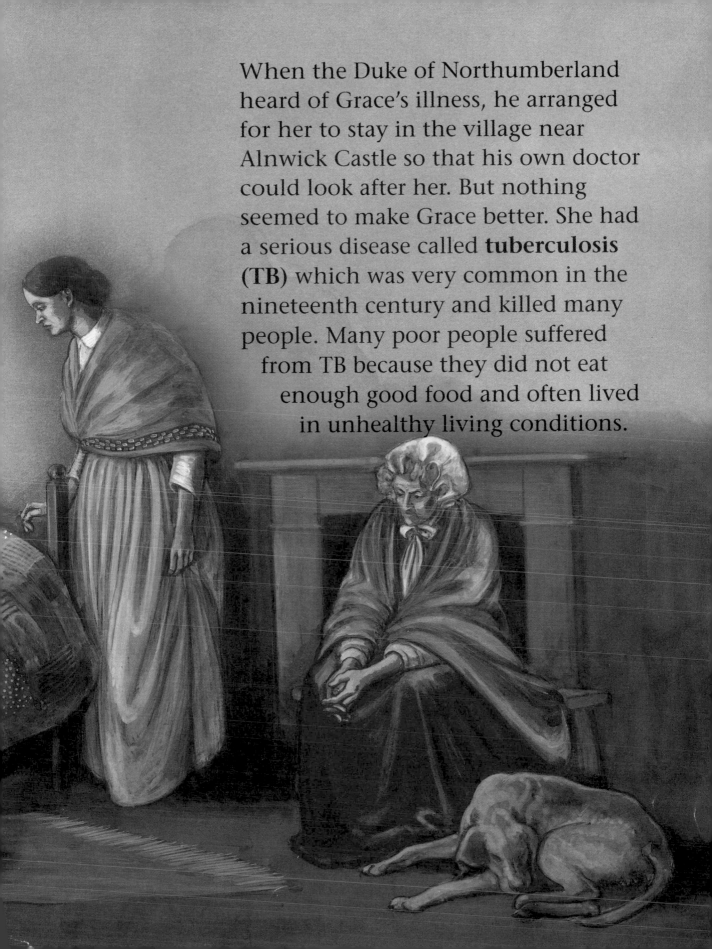

When the Duke of Northumberland heard of Grace's illness, he arranged for her to stay in the village near Alnwick Castle so that his own doctor could look after her. But nothing seemed to make Grace better. She had a serious disease called **tuberculosis (TB)** which was very common in the nineteenth century and killed many people. Many poor people suffered from TB because they did not eat enough good food and often lived in unhealthy living conditions.

As autumn drew on, Grace realized that she did not have long to live and she wrote to her mother and father. With her family gathered around her, Grace gave them each something from her collection of medals and presents. On 20 October 1842, at the age of twenty-seven, Grace died in her father's arms.

A horse-drawn hearse takes Grace's coffin past the crowds at her funeral. ▼

The funeral in Bamburgh was very grand. Hundreds of people, rich and poor, crowded the little village to say goodbye to Grace.

Two years later, a monument to Grace was put up in the churchyard overlooking the sea. It showed Grace lying down with an oar by her side.

Grace is remembered

Grace Darling was not forgotten by the **Victorians**. The famous poet, William Wordsworth, wrote a long poem about her. She was the subject of many books and a museum was built in Bamburgh in memory of her. The museum, which is still open today, has many of Grace's possessions. It has the boat she and her father used for the rescue and the clothes she was wearing on that day.

▲ Inside the Grace Darling Museum you can see Grace's dresses, shawls, bonnets and even locks of her hair.

There was also a popular song written about Grace which began:

'Twas on the Longstone lighthouse,
There dwelt an English maid:
Pure as the air around her,
Of danger ne'er afraid.
One morning just at daybreak,
A storm toss'd wreck she spied;
And tho' to try seemed madness,
"I'll save the crew!" she cried.'

Children visit Grace's monument, which was built two years after her death. ▼

Glossary

Crew The group of people in charge of a ship or plane.

Guardian Someone who protects or guides another person.

Heroine A very brave girl or woman.

Journal A diary.

Lighthouse A tall tower with a bright lamp at the top which guides and warns ships.

Maiden name A woman's surname before she is married.

Mainland A large area of land which is bigger than nearby islands.

Paddle-steamer A ship which is run by a steam engine. It has a huge wheel on each side which pushes it through the water.

Seamstress A woman who makes her living by sewing.

Spin To draw out and twist wool to make thread.

Spiral staircase A staircase which winds up in a circular shape from one room to another.

Steam engine An engine which uses steam to make it move.

Steamship Any ship which is run by a steam engine.

Tuberculosis (TB) A disease which usually attacks the lungs. It can now be cured by medicine.

Victorians The people who lived when Queen Victoria ruled Britain and Ireland (1837–1901).

Date chart

1815 September: William Darling is made lighthouse keeper on Brownsman Island.
24 November: Grace Darling is born in Bamburgh, Northumberland.
December: Grace is taken to live on Brownsman Island.
1826 The Darling family move to the lighthouse at Longstone Island.
1837 Victoria becomes Queen of Britain and Ireland.

1838 The *Forfarshire* is wrecked. Grace and William Darling save nine people.
The *Great Western* is built, the first steamship to regularly cross the Atlantic Ocean.
1842 April: Grace becomes ill with tuberculosis. She leaves Longstone Lighthouse to stay with her sister in Bamburgh.
20 October: Grace dies aged twenty-seven.

Books to read

Grace Darling by T. Hedge and T. Vicary (Oxford University Press, 1991)
History Storybook of Grace to the Rescue by M. Nash (Macdonald Young Books, 1995)
Ships, Sailors and the Sea by C. Young and J.C. Miles (Usborne, 1988)

Ships Through Time by Roy Richards (Macdonald Young Books, 1995)
Victorian Life series (Wayland, 1993–94)

Index

Picture acknowledgements
The publishers would like to thank the following for allowing their photographs to be used in this book: English Life 22; Ferens Art Gallery: Hull City Museums, Art Galleries and Archives 15; Grace Darling Museum/M. Scott Weightman 7, 28; Hulton Deutsch *Cover, title page,* 13, 20, 27; Stewart Bonney (News) Agency 4, 8, 9, 16; National Maritime Museum 11.